FOR NANNY AND GRANDAD, A CONSTANT SOURCE OF INSPIRATION AND LAUGHS.

FRESH PRINTS

WITHDRAWN

25 EASY AND ENTICING
PRINTING PROJECTS
TO MAKE AT HOME

Christine Leech

BARRON'S

Photography by Keiko Oikawa

CONTENTS

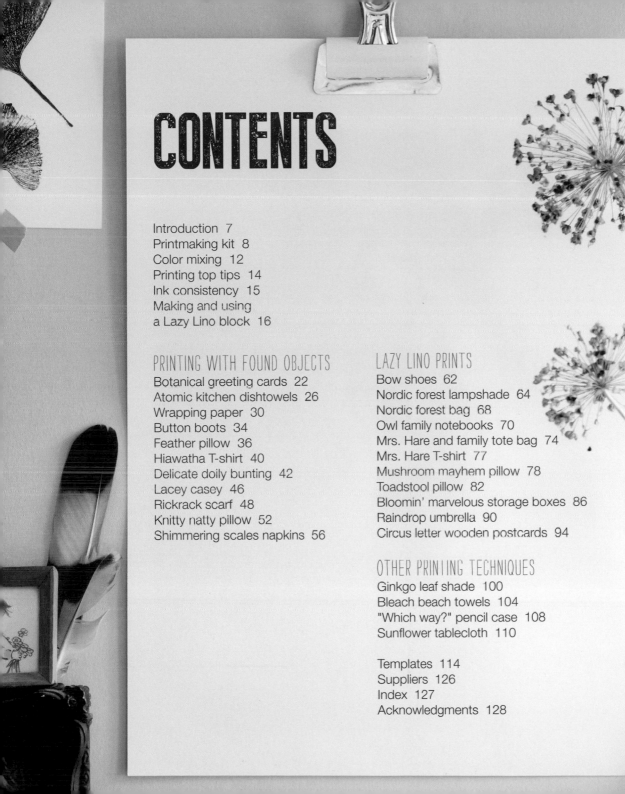

INTRODUCTION

When deciding where I was going to go to art college, I took two things into consideration: distance from home (not too far, not too close) and what the architecture of the buildings was like (old and crumbly good, modern and concrete bad). I remember visiting Bath School of Art and Design in England (where I eventually went on to study illustration) and walking into the two large printing studios—one for screen printing (where I maybe spent three days in the three years I was there) and one for everything else—woodcuts, lino cuts, engravings, litho prints, mono prints, and letterpress. The latter smelt of turps, fresh ink, and coffee and I fell instantly at home.

The majority of my final year show was made up of different forms of printing. Sadly, though, once I graduated and lost access to the beautiful old presses and endless supplies of ink, my printing days came to an end. So imagine how excited (and slightly concerned) I was when asked to do a book on printing. How would I decide what types of printing to use in my projects? What materials and tools would be available to the home printer? Fortunately, I needn't have worried. Having made the initial decision that the book would focus on block printing where different objects are used as printing blocks, be they found objects, such as cookie cutters or leaves, or engraved blocks of wood or lino, the ideas for projects quickly started taking shape.

I still had a slight concern, a worry for my (and your) fingers. My hands were always covered in small cuts and blisters from the engraving tools I used when making my woodcuts at college and I wanted to avoid this for the book if I could. And I have! Most of the projects on the following pages are made using craft foam sheets as the basis for the block.

This foam, which I have christened Lazy Lino, is a thin sheet of polystyrene that can be cut with scissors and indented ("engraved") with a pencil, giving all the detail of a woodcut but with much less risk to fingertips. It can be used on large-scale projects, such as the Mushroom Mayhem Pillow (see page 78), and on dainty intricate prints, such as the Mrs. Hare and Family Tote Bag (see page 74). It takes a fraction of the time to make and if your engraving tool slips or you cut the wrong piece out, you haven't just wasted four days of work as it's super quick to make another block.

The projects that don't use Lazy Lino use things that are readily available and are probably in your house right now—potato mashers, rickrack, buttons, and cookie cutters are all used for printing. They create surprising repeat patterns, such as on the Atomic Kitchen Dishtowels and Button Boots (see pages 26 and 34). You don't need many inks and you don't need a heavy press (a rolling pin works just as well). You just need some space, paper, and ideas.

As soon as I started on my first project, I remembered how exciting and addictive printing is and soon my kitchen floor was covered with my experiments. The whole day had flown by and the smell of fresh ink was everywhere. I hope you are inspired by the projects in this book; they really are fun to make and so simple.

Enjoy yourself (and don't forget to stop for lunch).

PRINTMAKING KIT

The printmaking room at college was my favorite place to work. I loved the smell, the giant pots of ink, and the anticipation I felt before I saw each print come off the press. My printmaking space at home isn't so grand, but it still smells the same and works just as well.

PRINTING INKS

There are lots of different types of inks on the market, ones that are specific to block printing or screen printing, stenciling, or litho. I've used the same ink on all the projects in this book and that is a fabric block printing ink manufactured by Speedball. It is a unique oil-based ink that cleans up easily with soap and water (so no messing around with smelly solvents). The ink comes in a variety of colors, including a metallic gold and silver (see also pages 12–13), and it's suitable for both fabric and paper.

If you are using it on fabrics, leave it for a week before the first wash. I've put several of my pieces through the washing machine at a low temperature and they came out fine. For a couple of the projects, I've used something different to print with. The Knitty Natty Pillow cover (see page 52) uses latex paint and the Bleach Beach Towels (see page 104) use household bleach.

OTHER USEFUL INKY THINGS

The temperature of your workspace can really affect the way your ink works. If the room is too hot, the ink will dry quickly on the plate. The way around this is to add a little ink retarder to your mix, which slows the drying time—particularly useful if you are working in a hot room. If you want to overprint colors to create the effect of extra colors,
then use a transparent extender base, which helps to make inks less opaque. For example, if you were to print a red triangle over a yellow square, where the colors overlap you will get an orangey hue.

BRAYERS (INK ROLLERS)

The brayers, or ink rollers, used to roll out the ink come in a variety of sizes. They range in price and quality and can get super expensive. I've acquired a variety over the years, such as a beautiful wood and brass-handled one with a durathene roller, which is quite small and so good for little blocks. The one I use the most has a 4" wide soft rubber roller and a plastic handle that I got from a general art store. It cleans up well and rolls the ink on smoothly and evenly. It's useful to have more than one brayer as it saves time if you need to have more than one color on the go. You can also use a clean brayer to apply pressure to the back of a block when you are printing.

PALETTE KNIVES

These long, flat, bendy metal artist's spatulas are great for mixing inks together, spreading ink out, and also scraping excess ink off the glass plate at the end of a job. There is something hypnotic about mixing colors together with a palette knife. If you don't have a palette knife, any wide bendy round-tipped metal spatula will work.

GLASS PLATE

You need a flat surface to mix and roll the inks out onto. A toughened glass plate is perfect. Alternatively, use a large smooth bathroom tile or a mirror tile. You can buy special ink-mixing trays that have a lip around the edge to stop the ink escaping, which is probably a wise precaution.

BAREN

A baren is a disk-shaped tool with a handle used to apply pressure to the back of your block so you get a nice even print. (See step 13 on page 18.)

ROLLING PIN

If you don't have a baren or you are printing a large print, then using a rolling pin over the back of the block is a good way to apply an even pressure. You can also use rolling pins for making repeat print patterns, such as on the Lacey Casey (see page 46).

SINK

A supply of running water and a sink is essential for printmaking, as there are times when it gets quite messy (or when you need to fill the kettle for a cup of tea). Most printing inks these days clean up with soap and warm water.

RAGS

When I was experimenting with the bleach patterns on the towels on page 104, I practiced on lots of cheap washcloths, which I now use constantly to clean up my inks, brayers, and glass plates. I also have a cheap pack of wipes that are really useful to remove the excess ink on the printing block or quickly clean up your fingers.

CLEAR PLASTIC BLOCKS

Different sizes of clear plastic (plexiglas) blocks make a good base for your Lazy Lino shapes. Because they are transparent, it's easy to line up the block when doing repeat prints or multicolored ones. You can buy them in a variety of ready-cut sizes from craft stores. If you are making oversize blocks, such as on the Knitty Natty Pillow (see page 52) or Rickrack Scarf (see page 48), then squares of thin fiberboard or thick, stiff cardboard work well.

MASKING TAPE

Use masking tape to fasten your sheet of Lazy Lino to the cutting mat when using a craft knife. This will stop the foam from slipping around and make it easier to cut. Masking tape is also invaluable for keeping the objects you are printing on flat and steady.

CRAFT FOAM SHEETS (AKA LAZY LINO)

Sheets of thin polystyrene for printing—called craft foam or "scratch" foam—come in 3–6 mm thicknesses and a range of sizes, starting at about 9" x 12". You can buy sheets with a self-adhesive back, which is useful for adhering to a clear plastic block, or you can just use double-sided tape, as I like to do. The foam is easy to make indentations in ("engrave") with a pencil or by pressing other objects into it. It is an inexpensive alternative to lino or wood. I have used Lazy Lino for all the block printing projects in this book.

LINO AND SOFT-CUT LINO

You can use soft-cut lino (Speedy-Carve) or lino to make your printing blocks, but you will need special lino cutting tools to engrave them, so they are a little more difficult to work with and a little more dangerous for your fingers. These blocks also take longer to prepare but the final block will last forever.

CRAFT KNIFE AND SCISSORS

Lazy Lino is easily cut with scissors or a craft knife. I prefer a knife as you can get a more intricate cut, but scissors are great too and safer for children.

METAL RULER

It's easier to cut a straight line with a metal ruler. Fact.

CUTTING MAT

Use a cutting mat so that you don't engrave your work surface with lines and patterns from the craft knife.

DOUBLE-SIDED TAPE

Use this to fix Lazy Lino to a clear plastic block.

PENCILS AND PENS

As Lazy Lino marks so easily, it's best to experiment with a range of pencils and pens to see which one makes the type of line and pattern indentations you like the most. I use a sharp (but not too sharp) pencil and a propelling pencil if I want a super-fine line (see also page 14).

LIGHTER FLUID

Use a little of this on a tissue or rag to clean leftover bits of double-sided tape from a clear plastic block before reusing it (see page 14). It leaves a little residue, so polish the plastic with a clean cloth afterward. Always keep lighter fluid in a safe place and clearly marked, as it can be harmful if inhaled or swallowed.

NEWSPRINT

I bought a big pack of newsprint (type of paper used for newspapers) before I started this book. It's great to test prints out on and also to protect floors and table tops.

PAPER

It's fun to experiment with printing on all kinds of paper, as each one gives a different effect. I love brown paper, and tracing paper can give some layered effects. If you want to make simple art prints with your blocks, then a smooth heavyweight drawing paper works well.

FABRIC CARE

The Speedball printing inks I've used on the projects are perfect for cotton, polyester, blends, linen, rayon, and other synthetic fibers but aren't great on nylon. I have also used them on velvet pillow covers and fabric-covered boxes, stretchy T-shirts, and canvas shoes. Leave your printed fabric for a week before washing and use a low temperature and mild laundry soap when putting it through the washing machine.

CARBON PAPER

Useful if you aren't confident about transferring the patterns onto the Lazy Lino (see page 14 for how to use the carbon paper).

FABRIC-COVERED BOARD

Sometimes when printing on fabric you get a better print if you print onto a slightly padded surface. This isn't always the case though, so it's good to experiment with a fabric scrap first.

It's easy to make a padded board—take a piece of fiberboard measuring about 20" x 28" (to stretch a T-shirt over), pieces of batting and cotton fabric that are large enough to stretch over the board, and a staple gun. Stretch the batting over the board and staple gun it in place on the back. Repeat with the cotton fabric and you're done.

WHITE CRAFT GLUE

Thick white waterproof craft glue that turns clear when dry can be used to hold the surface used for printing to the block and also to protect it from soaking up too much ink (see the Delicate Doily Bunting and Lacey Casey on pages 42 and 46). When covering a surface in glue, use an old stubby paintbrush to get the glue into all the nooks and crannies and leave to dry overnight. It can also be used to make printing lines, as on the Sunflower Tablecloth on page 110. Used as a drawing tool by squeezing the glue from the nozzle, like decorating a cake, it dries in a raised line that can then be printed from.

STRING

String is another useful material for making printing blocks with. Wound into patterns on a piece of cardboard or wood covered in white craft glue, it produces an attractive effect when printed (see the Ginkgo Leaf Shade on page 100).

COLOR MIXING

We are taught in school that red, yellow, and blue are the primary colors. These are colors that cannot be created by mixing other colors together, but when they themselves are mixed together you can create a range of other colors.

These three colors are super useful; you can get away with just buying these plus white and black when looking to purchase inks for your printing projects. However, if you add in a tube of magenta and a tube of turquoise, suddenly you have a lot more subtle changes in color at your disposal. Printing inks also come in a variety of ready-mixed colors, each one a strong vibrant shade. The inks I've used on the projects in this book come in a range of 13 different colors, including gold and silver, but it's my tubes of white, turquoise, magenta, yellow, blue, and red that are almost empty.

The illustrations on these pages show what happens when you mix certain colors together. But be prepared to experiment; the tiniest change in quantity of color can really affect the shades you create.

MIXING COLOR TOP TIPS

1 When trying to mix a new hue, start by squeezing a little of each color you are going to use onto a sheet of scrap paper. Mix them together with your finger until you have the right shade, remembering the rough amount of each color used (for example, you may have used twice as much red as yellow to make a particular shade of orange). Once you are happy with a color, then you can mix it on a large scale.

2 Use white to make a color lighter, but using black to make a color darker often kills the color and makes it dull. So use the tiniest bit as it is so powerful or use other colors to make the shade darker (browns, blues, greens, and reds all help).

3 If you want a pale color, add a little of the color to white rather than the other way round.

4 Darker colors have the most pigment in them, so you often need less of them. Mix them in a little at a time.

1 PART YELLOW + 1 PART RED = ORANGE

1 PART YELLOW + 1 PART TURQUOISE + 1 PART RED = OLIVE

1 PART WHITE + 1 PART YELLOW = LEMON YELLOW

1 PART YELLOW + 1 PART BLUE = GREEN

1 PART YELLOW + 1 PART TURQUOISE + 1 PART RED + ½ PART WHITE = PALE OLIVE

1 PART BROWN + 1 PART WHITE + 1 PART YELLOW = OCHER

5 There are some colors that are trickier than others to mix. I spent hours trying to make up olives, ochers, and grays (without using black). In the end, I found a tube of ready-mixed brown ink really helped.

6 To inject a little bit of sparkle, add metallic silver or gold to your colors.

MIXING UP THE INK

When you have worked out the correct color combination to create your desired shade, start mixing the inks together on your plate of glass using a palette knife. Work at the top of the glass plate so you have space to roll the ink out later. Swipe the knife back and forth blending the inks, then scrape up all the ink and dollop it back down on the glass and swipe again. It's a lovely thing to watch the colors blending. When the colors are well blended, use the brayer to roll out a layer of ink in the lower half of the glass plate (for information on ink consistency, see page 15). To ensure the colors are fully mixed together, roll the ink out left to right, then up and down. Don't try to roll out all the ink at once because it will dry out quickly. Instead, leave a reserve of ink at the top of the glass plate.

1 PART WHITE + 1 PART TURQUOISE = PALE TURQUOISE

1 PART WHITE + 1 PART BLUE = WEDGWOOD BLUE

1 PART MAGENTA + 1 PART BLUE + 1 PART WHITE = LILAC

1 PART BROWN + 1 PART WHITE + 1 PART BLUE = STEEL GRAY

1 PART TURQUOISE + 1 PART BLUE = TEAL

2 PARTS GREEN + 1 PART BLACK = DARK GREEN

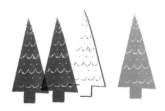

2 PARTS BLACK + 1 PART WHITE = DARK GRAY

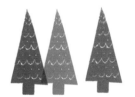

1 PART RED + 1 PART BLUE = PURPLE

1 PART MAGENTA + 1 PART WHITE = PALE PINK

TOP TIP

Sometimes you might not want to completely mix your inks together. You can get an attractive ombré effect if you only blend your inks in one direction.

13

PRINTING TOP TIPS

USING PLASTIC BLOCKS

The advantage of using a clear plastic (plexiglas) block as a base for your Lazy Lino, rather than a piece of fiberboard, is that if you are making a multicolored print, being able to see through the plastic when lining up the block makes it much easier to get a perfect print. They are also easier to clean and reuse. Many craft stores sell clear plastic blocks with grooves down the side for your fingers. I bought several of mine on eBay. An even less expensive option is to get a large plastic sheet and cut it into pieces.

To clean leftover double-sided tape from your plastic blocks before using them again, use lighter fluid. First remove as much of the Lazy Lino from the block as you can using your fingers, then wash the remaining ink away with warm soapy water. Any sticky bits left on the blocks will come off with a squirt of lighter fluid and a rub with a rag.

TRANSFERRING PATTERNS

Use carbon paper to transfer a pattern from a template to the Lazy Lino. Place a piece of the carbon paper between the template and the Lazy Lino, carbon-side down, and draw over the template with a pencil (and a light touch) to transfer the pattern onto the foam.

There are also lots of doodlesque patterns in this book, which are made up of simple lines, dots, dashes, hearts, and scallops. I've drawn the patterns clearly on the templates so they should be easy to copy (see pages 114–125).

MAKING INDENTATIONS

I tried a whole host of pens, pencils, pins, and pointy things when looking for the best tool to make indentations in the Lazy Lino. I found one pencil that worked well, not too sharp and not too blunt; it didn't tear up the foam, but left a nice crisp line. Perfect! For super-fine lines I found the tip of a propelling pencil was great, but be careful, because if your lines are too fine, they will fill in with ink.

When making marks, don't press too hard as the foam is so soft, a little pressure is enough to get a good indentation. The harder you press, the wider your pattern will be when you come to print. So again, experiment until you find a pressure and a result you're happy with.

MAKING PRINTS

Always do a test print of your block before printing onto your chosen surface. This not only allows you to work out the pressure you need to apply to get an even print, but shows if there is anywhere that could use a deeper indentation to get a clear pattern. Also, you often get a better print the second or third time as, by then, there is a good base layer of ink on the block.

MAKING ENDURING BLOCKS

I could only find one slight downside to using Lazy Lino instead of a more substantial carving block. Because the foam is quite thin, over time the edges of your print and the marked pattern can lose their crispness. When doing more frequent pattern repeats (like on the Nordic Forest Lampshade on page 64), you may need to make new Lazy Lino shapes during the project. For a longer-lasting block, all the Lazy Lino blocks in this book can easily be cut from lino, soft-cut lino, or wood.

INK CONSISTENCY

Each printing material requires a different consistency of ink to get the best print. Lazy Lino prints require a fine consistency, while potato and found object printing need a medium consistency, and blocks made from fabric (such as the Delicate Doily Bunting on page 42) use a thicker consistency.

I usually squeeze out about 1¼" of ink when starting a project. I find this is enough to get a good layer of ink rolled out and several prints done with not too much ink wasted at the end. Obviously this all depends on the size of the block you are printing and how many times you use it. (Is it a repeat pattern? Are you printing all your Christmas cards at once?) As you get used to using the ink, you will be able to tell roughly how much ink you need for a project.

THICK CONSISTENCY

1 Squeeze out the ink at the top of the glass plate to allow space to roll out the ink into the necessary consistency. For a thick consistency, you usually have to only roll the ink a couple of times. The ink forms large peaks on the glass plate and brayer as you roll and it sounds very squelchy.

MEDIUM CONSISTENCY

2 If you are printing on fabric or with a large block, then a medium consistency is good. Roll the ink out over a larger area of the glass plate to get this consistency. The peaks are smaller and it begins to feel quite tacky.

THIN CONSISTENCY

3 Printing with smaller foam blocks and on paper usually requires a thin consistency of ink (if the ink is too thick, then your block may slip on the paper and the etched lines may fill in). Roll the ink down the glass plate until you have a fine layer of ink. If you roll the ink out too fine, use a palette knife to scrape all the ink together and start again.

MAKING AND USING A LAZY LINO BLOCK

Remember that printing works with reversed images. So to make sure your image faces the right way when printed; it needs to be stuck to your block back to front. This means that any words you use need to be drawn in reverse … tricky.

SUPPLIES

Pencil

Sheet of craft foam (Lazy Lino)

Masking tape

Cutting mat

Craft knife

Metal ruler

Double-sided tape

Clear plastic block

Printing ink

Palette knife

Glass plate

Brayer (ink roller)

Baren or rolling pin

1 Copy your chosen template onto white paper (I've used a Nordic Forest tree from page 123 here). Using masking tape, stick the template to a similar size piece of foam. Then tape them both to your cutting mat to stop the Lazy Lino from moving around, which makes it easier to cut intricate shapes.

2 Using a craft knife (and ruler if necessary), cut away the excess Lazy Lino. If your shape has curved sides, it's easier to cut it away in sections than doing it all at once.

3 Remove the shape (a tree here) from the excess Lazy Lino.

4 Use a pencil to mark any decorations on your shape. You don't have to press hard to get an indentation.

5 Repeat steps 1–4 with the rest of the pieces that you need for your project.

6 Place strips of double-sided tape over the back of the shape. It doesn't have to be completely covered, but make sure all the important areas, including narrow parts, are taped. (If you are using a foam sheet with an adhesive back, you can bypass this step.)

7 Remove the paper backing from the tape (or foam) and place the shape on a suitably sized clear plastic block. If you are printing several colors in one project (such as for the Bloomin' Marvelous Storage Boxes on page 86) make up a block for each of the colors.

8 Squeeze out your chosen inks onto the glass plate and use a palette knife to start blending the inks together (see pages 12–13 for color mixing tips).

CONT. >>>

9 Roll out the ink with a brayer to get an even coverage, rolling first one way, then the other. Make an appropriate consistency of ink, as described in each project and on page 15.

10 When you have rolled the ink to the right consistency, start rolling up your block. Make sure all the Lazy Lino is covered.

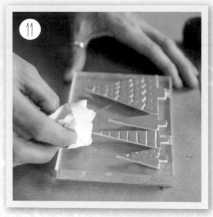

11 If you have got any ink on the clear plastic block, wipe it away with a tissue or damp cloth and make sure your fingers are clean, too—you don't want to ruin your masterpiece with fingerprints.

12 Carefully place the block face down on the surface you are printing on. Press gently on the back of the block with your fingers to fix it in place.

13 Use the baren or rolling pin (or your fingers) to apply an even pressure across the whole back of the block.

14 Lift the block from the printed surface. Ta-dah!

CHAPTER 1

PRINTING WITH FOUND OBJECTS

Wherever you are sitting reading this book there is probably something within your eyesight that would make a good printing block. Be it a potato, a potato masher, a button, a bowl, or a bracelet, anything that has a texture on it or an interesting shape will do. When covered with ink and rolled, pressed, or stamped onto a surface, it will leave some kind of imprint behind. It may be an amazingly detailed print from feathers and leaves or a bold repeat pattern from kitchen cutlery. Whatever it is, it will be fun experimenting.

• Botanical Greeting Cards • Atomic Kitchen Dishtowels
• Wrapping Paper • Button Boots • Feather Pillow
• Hiawatha T-shirt • Delicate Doily Bunting
• Lacey Casey • Rickrack Scarf • Knitty Natty Pillow
• Shimmering Scales Napkins

BOTANICAL GREETING CARDS

Certain leaves and feathers make amazing prints. They are so detailed that they look like an incredible Victorian etching, but the printing process is probably one of the simplest there is.

SUPPLIES

Black printing ink

Two glass plates

Brayer (ink roller)

A selection of feathers and leaves

Plain blank greeting cards

Paper towels

Rolling pin or second brayer

There is such a variety of textures in nature, all perfect for some experimental printing. I've found the best leaves to print are ones that aren't too fleshy and have a good grain or vein structure. Often the underside of a leaf has more prominent veins, so use this side to take the print from. Ferns, feathers, and ginkgo leaves work well, but as soon as you start this project, I bet you will be wanting to print with your whole garden.

1 Squeeze some black ink onto one of the glass plates and roll it out to a fine consistency (see page 15). Make sure the brayer is coated with a thin layer of ink. Place the feather or leaf on the second glass plate and gently roll over it with the brayer.

2 Make sure the feather is all covered with ink and then carefully lift it off the glass plate.

CONT. >>>

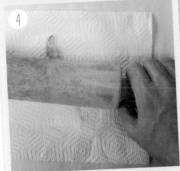

》》》

3   Place the unfolded greeting card on a flat surface and position the inked-up feather on the card, ink-side down.

4   Lay a sheet of paper towel over the feather and card and gently (so as not to move the feather) but firmly (to apply some pressure), roll over the feather and paper towel using a rolling pin or clean brayer.

5   Carefully remove the paper towel and feather to reveal the print.

EXTRA!

Instead of printing greeting cards, why not try a larger feather or a variety of leaves to print a picture for your wall.

I rolled some gold ink onto the tip of the feather below before I printed it to make this beautiful two toned effect.

Make a negative print by placing the feather or leaf onto the card and roll over it once with an inked brayer. This will leave a silhouette on the card. If you then roll the brayer across another piece of paper, you will get a print of the feather from the brayer.

ATOMIC KITCHEN DISHTOWELS

★ ★

The prints on these dishtowels are all made using a variety of kitchen utensils and other household items. The ink colors give them a cool retro feel.

Plain white dishtowels, washed and ironed

Masking tape

Black, pale turquoise, and ocher printing inks (see pages 12–13 for color mixing tips)

Palette knife

Glass plate

Brayer (ink roller)

Sandpaper (optional)

Variety of kitchen utensils and household items (see diagrams on page 28 for specifics)

1 It's amazing what you can find around the house that makes a good print! On these dishtowels I've used a potato masher, a sink drainer, some cookie cutters, a bottle top, a couple of frosting nozzles, a wooden spatula, a fork, and a wooden clothespin. Follow the patterns I've made or create your own.

2 Lay a dishtowel on a flat surface and tape it down at the corners so it is nice and flat.

3 Choose which dishtowel design you wish to print first (see your choices on page 28) and follow the instructions on the appropriate illustration.

4 Mix up each ink on the glass plate and roll out to a medium consistency (see page 15). If the ink doesn't stick to a utensil very well, rub a little sandpaper over it (before you ink it up!) and also let the ink dry slightly before printing.

CONT. ⟩⟩⟩

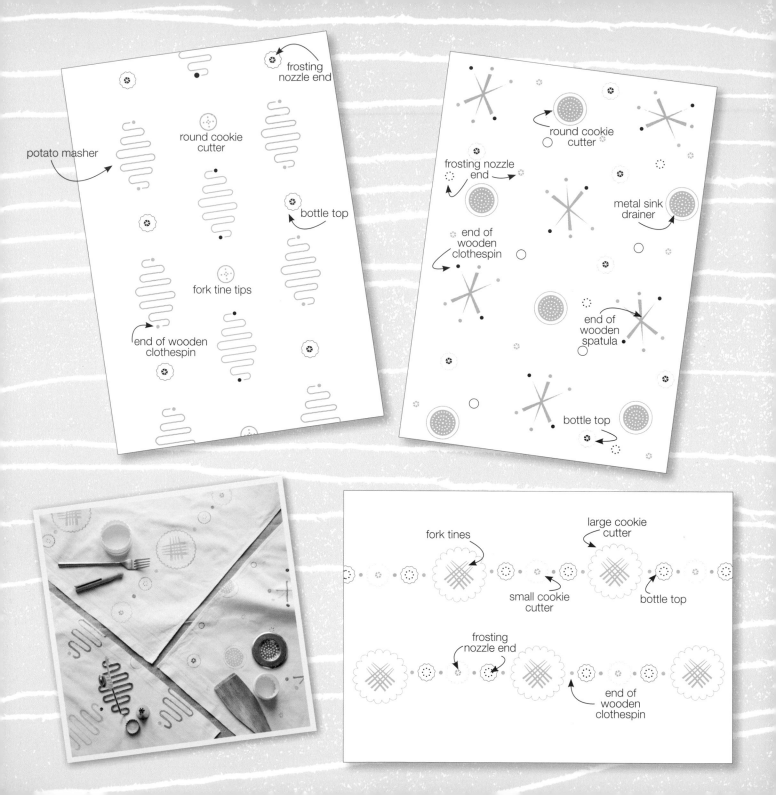

EXTRA! INSTEAD OF PRINTING WITH KITCHEN UTENSILS, USE NOVELTY KITCHEN OR BATHROOM SPONGES TO PRINT BOLD AND COLORFUL PATTERNS.

WRAPPING PAPER

White ink and glitter give the humble brown craft paper used for this project a stylish look. Follow these steps and you too can make expensive looking wrapping paper quickly and cheaply.

SUPPLIES

Potato or sweet potato

Vegetable knife

Cookie (or frosting) cutters in three sizes

Paper towels

Roll of brown craft paper

Masking tape (optional)

White printing ink

Glass plate

Brayer (ink roller)

White craft glue

Glitter

1 yard of ribbon, $^1/_2$–$^3/_4$" wide

TO PREPARE THE FLOWERS

1 Cut the potato in half so you have an area of flat potato large enough for the cookie cutter to sit on it easily. Cut a slice off the base of the potato to make it sit flat on your work surface.

2 Press the cookie cutter into the potato to mark the shape.

3 Use the vegetable knife to cut away the excess potato so the shape left by the cutter protrudes by about $^1/_2$". Repeat with other cutters for different sizes.

4 If you are using a normal potato, dry the cut surface off by dabbing it with a piece of paper towel and leaving it to dry out while you prepare the ink and paper. Stick a fork into the back of the potato, which helps with moving the potatoes around when printing.

CONT. >>>

>>>

TO PRINT ON THE PAPER

5 Roll out 1 yard of brown paper onto a flat surface covered in newspaper (to collect the glitter). If it tends to roll back up, fasten it down at the edges with masking tape.

6 Squeeze some white ink onto the glass plate and roll it out to a medium consistency (see page 15). Then use the brayer to roll the ink onto the potatoes and start printing.

7 To make the outline flower shapes, print using the cookie cutters with ink rolled onto their surface.

8 Print the largest flower shapes first, using both the potato and the cutter and printing in a random pattern over the paper. Then fill in the rest of the paper with the medium and smaller shapes.

9 Overlap the cutters and potatoes to get more intricate flower shapes.

10 To make the glitter shapes, print with white craft glue instead of ink and then sprinkle a generous amount of glitter over the area. When finished, lift the wrapping paper up and collect the glitter on the newspaper below.

11 Print the gift tags in a similar way. If you are making glitter tags then it can be easier to gently press the glued tag into a pile of glitter.

TO PRINT ON THE RIBBON

12 Lay the ribbon out flat and tape it down at the ends. Print along the length of the ribbon, alternating between ink and glue. Sprinkle glitter as before onto the glue and shake off.

ALSO LOOKS GOOD ON ...

Greeting cards: Make a range of goodies by printing several greeting cards while you are making the wrapping paper.

BUTTON BOOTS

Printing with buttons gives a quirky alternative to a polka dot print. One color makes them more sophisticated, but more colors = more fun!

SUPPLIES

Thin cardboard

Pair of canvas shoes

Masking tape

Various buttons

Sandpaper (optional)

Gray and orange printing inks (see pages 12–13 for color mixing tips)

Palette knife

Glass plate

Brayer (ink roller)

Double-sided tape

1 Make two rough semicircles from the cardboard to place inside the toes of your shoes. This gives a firmer base to print onto. Also stick some tape around the rubber edge and remove any shoe laces.

2 Choose a variety of buttons in different shapes and sizes. The buttons that work best are ones that have a very flat side and no indentations or ridges. If they are shiny, give them a light rub with sandpaper on the flat side to help the ink adhere better.

3 Mix up a gray ink on the glass plate and roll it out to a fine consistency (see page 15).

4 The best way to get firm and even pressure on the button is to stick it directly to your index finger using double-sided tape.

5 Roll the ink onto the button and begin printing. To get a good print, use your index finger and thumb in a pinching action with the boot fabric in between you finger, pressing the fabric onto the button. Swap buttons occasionally so you get an attractive random pattern.

6 Roll out some orange ink and print a few buttons to add color. Leave to dry overnight.

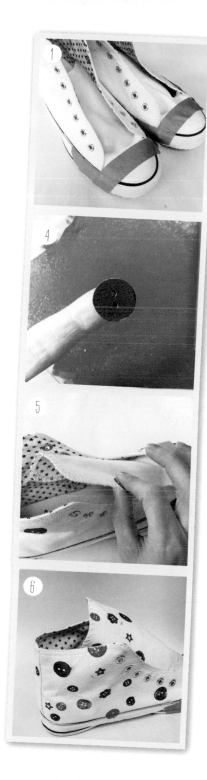

FEATHER PILLOW

Sweet potatoes are the perfect shape to make feather prints from. They have a lower water content than potatoes so you can get a crisper print. The velvet nap on this pillow gives the print a silvery glow.

Sweet potatoes

Vegetable knife

Colored pencil

Lino cutting tool

Forks

White, pink, orange, turquoise, green, purple, and gold printing inks (see pages 12–13 for color mixing tips)

Palette knife

Glass plate

Brayer (ink roller)

Velvet pillow cover and a pillow form

Masking tape

TO PREPARE THE FEATHERS

1 Slice the sweet potatoes in half lengthwise.

2 Use a colored pencil to draw a rough guide of the feather on the potato. Follow the illustrations below and the feathers on the finished pillow for ideas for your feather shapes.

3 Use the vegetable knife to cut and trim the stalk of the feather.

4 Take the lino cutting tool and carefully cut channels in the potato to represent the central stem and the feathers. Cut one long channel down the center and then several fanning off from this on either side in random groups.

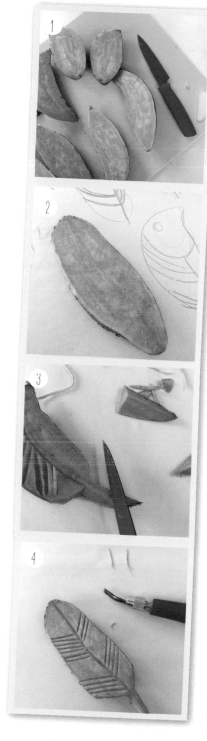

CONT. >>>

5 Repeat steps 2–4 on five other halves. You can use the knife to shape the whole potato if you are not happy with the natural shape.

TO PRINT ON THE PILLOW COVER

6 Stick a fork in the backs of the potatoes to make them easier to handle and so you can apply more pressure when printing. On the glass plate, roll out the white ink to a medium consistency (see page 15), then ink up the potato halves.

7 Lay the pillow cover on a flat surface. Tape the edges down so it can't move around. Start in one corner of the pillow and begin printing by placing the potatoes in a random pattern. Try to make the feathers curve into one another. You can probably get at least two printings from each inking of a potato. The second inking will be paler than the first, but this gives an airy feel to the design.

8 Continue until the whole pillow cover is filled.

9 To print the colored tips, clean up the potatoes and cut each tip of them off in a V-shape. Stick a fork in the backs of these, too.

10 Roll out the colored inks to a medium consistency and print by matching up the feather tips with their corresponding feather.

11 Leave the cover to dry before stuffing with a pillow form.

EXTRA! PRINT THESE FEATHERS IN WHITE INK ONTO A WHITE WINDOW SHADE FOR A SUBTLE BUT BEAUTIFUL LOOK, ESPECIALLY WHEN THE SUN SHINES IN.

HIAWATHA T-SHIRT

This T-shirt uses the same sweet potato printing technique as the Feather Pillow on pages 36–39.

 SUPPLIES

T-shirt, washed and ironed

Masking tape

Sweet potatoes

Vegetable knife

Colored pencil

Lino cutting tool

Forks

White, magenta, orange, green, and dark green printing inks (see pages 12–13 for color mixing tips)

Palette knife

Glass plate

Brayer (ink roller)

1 Place the T-shirt on a flat surface and tape it down.

2 Follow steps 1–4 of the Feather Pillow (see page 37) for making the potato feathers. You need to make four feathers ranging in size from approximately 2 1/2" to 4 3/4".

3 Mix up some orange ink on the glass plate and roll out to a medium consistency (see page 15). Start with the largest feather and print it on the center of the neckline of the T-shirt. Roll the ink onto the potato so you get an even covering. Work out from this feather printing the rest of the feathers in different colored inks. On the back of the T-shirt I included a leaf in a paler green than the one on the front.

4 Use smaller feathers each time and work symmetrically around the neckline. Leave the T-shirt to dry.

ALSO LOOKS GOOD ON ...

Tote bags: Try a repeat pattern of the same feather in one color or a random pattern like the pillow cover on the previous page.

40

DELICATE DOILY BUNTING

An intricate lace doily makes a beautiful printing block, giving an amazingly delicate print that produces a nice alternative to traditional bunting.

1¼ yard of white cotton fabric, 44" wide

Piece of thin fiberboard (or thick, stiff cardboard), ¾" larger all around than the doily

White craft glue

Old paintbrush

Lace doily

Pink and white printing inks (see pages 12–13 for color mixing tips)

Palette knife

Glass plate

Brayer (ink roller)

Rolling pin

Pinking shears

Scissors

1 yard of narrow white ribbon

Sewing machine

TO PREPARE THE FABRIC

1 Cut the white cotton fabric into squares the same size as the fiberboard (or cardboard) block.

TO PREPARE THE DOILY BLOCK

2 Cover the fiberboard with glue and use the paintbrush to spread it across the block.

3 Place the doily on the glued surface and use the brush in a downward dabbing motion to firmly stick the doily to the block. Add more glue to the top of the doily and get it into all the nooks and crannies. Leave the doily to dry completely—ideally overnight.

TO PRINT ON THE FABRIC

4 Mix up some pink ink on the glass plate and roll it out to a medium consistency (see page 15). Don't worry about mixing enough ink to print all your fabric at once—the variety of shades of pink mixed in each batch gives a pretty ombré effect.

5 Roll up the doily with the ink and wipe away any that gets onto the block.

6 Place a piece of cotton fabric on the doily block and use a rolling pin to apply even pressure to the fabric. Carefully peel the fabric from the block and leave it to dry.

7 Ink up the doily block after each print. The first two or three prints may be a bit pale as the ink takes time to infiltrate the doily, but after the first few you will get an amazingly detailed print.

8 When all the prints are dry carefully cut around each doily with the pinking shears, leaving about a 1/2" border all around. Then cut each one in half using normal scissors.

TO MAKE THE BUNTING

9 Pile all the doily halves together and use a sewing machine set to a simple straight stitch to join them together. Run each doily half through the machine about 1/4" from the straight edge of the doily and butting the next one up to it as you go. Alternatively, you can hand sew the doily halves together with a couple of stitches at each side.

10 Cut the white ribbon in half. Fold one piece in the middle and stitch this fold to one end of the bunting. Repeat on the other end.

11 Hang your colorful bunting somewhere nice.

ALSO LOOKS GOOD ON ...

Table linen: Using the same doily (or a mixture of two or three) to print on coasters, napkins, and place mats allows you to make a whole set of tablecloths cheaply. Try printing on felt or other non-fraying fabric so that you don't have to hem the finished articles.

LACEY CASEY

Using a rolling pin as a printing tool is an easy way to not only get a repeat pattern but also a cool graduated ombré effect.

Pieces of lace trimming, the circumference of the rolling pin and a similar thickness so they print evenly

White craft glue

Wooden rolling pin

White and Wedgwood blue printing inks (see pages 12–13 for color mixing tips)

Palette knife

Glass plate

Brayer (ink roller)

Pair of pillowcases, washed and ironed

Masking tape

TO PREPARE THE LACE BLOCK

1   Choose a selection of lace and ribbons to make up the pattern on your rolling pin. The lace that works best has a pronounced pattern and is quite thick.

2   Cover the rolling pin in white craft glue. Then wrap the lace around the rolling pin and press it into place. Cut away any excess so it fits neatly together. Repeat with any other lace or ribbon you have to create a wider pattern on the rolling pin.

3   Cover all the fabric with more glue, making sure no fabric is left unglued. Try to make the lace and ribbon as straight as possible going around the pin, then leave to dry overnight.

TO PRINT ON THE PILLOWCASE

4   Mix up some Wedgwood blue ink on the glass plate and roll it out to a medium consistency (see page 15). Ink up the rolling pin, covering the lace completely. Then roll twice on some scrap fabric so the ink soaks into the lace completely.

5   Tape one of the pillowcases to a flat surface. Roll the rolling pin over the pillowcase in one smooth firm roll. Repeat with the other pillowcase and leave to dry.

RICKRACK SCARF

Make a big print block using strips of rickrack and you can quickly cover large areas, such as on this scarf. Don't worry about the lines of rickrack being super straight—a little uneven looks good, too.

Thick, stiff cardboard or 5 mm-thick foam artboard

Scissors

White craft glue

4¼ yards of rickrack, ½" wide

Old paintbrush

Rolling pin

Yellow and white printing inks

Palette knife

Glass plate

Brayer (ink roller)

Plain cotton scarf, or thin fabric, measuring approximately 24" x 70"

Scrap of fabric for testing

EXTRA!

Make a gingham effect by printing one color vertically and the other horizontally across the scarf.

Buy different widths of rickrack trim for a varied look.

TO PREPARE THE RICKRACK BLOCK

1 Cut a piece of cardboard so that its shorter sides are the same as the length of your rolling pin and its longer sides are the same as the width of your scarf.

2 Straight from the tube, dribble 5–6 lines of white craft glue onto the cardboard parallel to the longer side, widely spaced apart and with some traveling at slight diagonals and some straight.

3 Cut the rickrack into pieces the same length as the glue lines. Place each piece on the cardboard over one of the lines of glue and run another line of glue over the top. Use an old paintbrush to dab the glue firmly over the rickrack and cardboard, making sure the rickrack remains as straight as possible. Repeat until the cardboard is full. Leave to dry fully—ideally overnight.

CONT. >>>

TO PRINT ON THE SCARF

4 Mix a little white ink with the yellow to make it paler on the glass plate and roll out to a thick consistency (see page 15). Roll the ink onto the rickrack block and use a tissue or rag to wipe away any ink that gets onto the cardboard. Pay special attention to the edges.

5 Do a couple of test prints on some old fabric first—this allows the ink time to get right into the rickrack giving a more consistent print and also allows you to work out how much pressure you have to apply. Place the block face down on the scrap fabric, use your hands to press it onto the fabric to stop it from moving, then roll firmly over it a couple of times with the rolling pin. Carefully lift the block from the fabric.

6 Lay the scarf out on a flat surface. You may have to print it in a couple of sections unless you have a really long table!

7 Ink up the block and place it on the fabric. Draw an arrow on the back of the cardboard pointing in the direction of the majority of fabric. This will help you place the block down the right way every time.

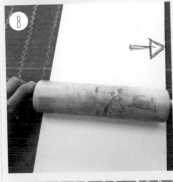

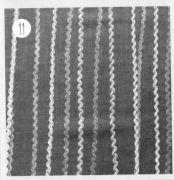

8 Use the rolling pin to apply even firm pressure across the block.

9 Carefully lift the block from the scarf. Repeat steps 8–9 until the whole scarf is covered.

10 Clean as much of the yellow ink from the block and leave it to dry, then ink it up with white ink.

11 You can either lay the block down in the same direction as you did with the yellow ink or flip it so the arrow is facing the other way. Whichever you choose, make sure you start with the block as you can set slightly farther up the fabric so you can see the first yellow line and make the rickrack lines staggered. Practice which way you like best with the scrap piece of fabric.

12 Print the whole scarf with the white ink and then leave it overnight to dry.

ALSO LOOKS GOOD ON

A simple white T-shirt: A blue print is an attractive alternative to the traditional Breton top.

Drum lampshade: Run the rickrack stripes vertically around a lampshade (see page 64 for more instructions).

KNITTY NATTY PILLOW

This print miraculously transforms a sewn fabric pillow cover into a knitted pillow cover. If you have any leftover paint from home renovations, you can use it to make perfectly matched pillow covers for your newly decorated room.

SUPPLIES

Old knitted sweater worked in bulky yarn

16" square pillow cover, washed and ironed, and a pillow form

Scissors

Square of thin fiberboard, 8" x 8"

White craft glue and old paintbrush

Pale gray latex paint

Glass plate

Two brayers (ink rollers)

Piece of thick cardboard, 20" x 20"

Baren or rolling pin

TIPS BEFORE PRINTING

The kinds of knitted sweaters that work best for this project are cotton or not too fluffy wool ones with a strongly pronounced stitch pattern—large cables are particularly effective. Scour thrift stores or yard sales for a sweater.

Mounting the knitting onto a piece of wood and covering it with white craft glue makes the stitches stand out more, and means you can apply an even pressure when printing.

TO PREPARE THE KNITTING BLOCK

1. Lay the sweater on a flat surface. Choose one 8" square area that will work best as the print, then cut out. The pillow shown opposite uses two different sections of knitting, but it works equally as well with just one.

2. Cover the fiberboard with an even thick layer of white craft glue. Place the square of knitting face up on the fiberboard and arrange it so the side edges are neat and straight. Knitting has a tendency to move around once cut, so you may have to trim the sides to neaten them. Press down the knitting into the glue using the paintbrush.

3. Spread more glue on top of the knitting, then use the paintbrush to ensure that the adhesive covers the whole square.

CONT. >>>

》》》

4 Use a firm downward dabbing motion to completely coat the knitting. Leave to dry overnight.

TO PRINT ON THE PILLOW COVER

5 Place the pillow cover on the cardboard.

6 Pour a quantity of paint onto the glass plate; a line about 6" long and 2" wide should be sufficient. Roll the paint out to coat the brayer evenly, then roll up the knitting block. Coat the block evenly and until all of the knitting is covered.

7 Place the block face down on one corner of the pillow cover and press firmly using a baren or rolling pin.

8 Place one hand on top of the block and pillow cover and slide the other under the cardboard and flip everything over. Be careful not to allow the fabric or block to move. Remove the cardboard and use the clean brayer to press the fabric into the printing block. Carefully remove the pillow cover from the block.

9 Repeat steps 5–8 three more times in the other corners of the pillow cover. Rotating the block gives a patchwork effect. Leave the cover to dry before filling with a pillow form.

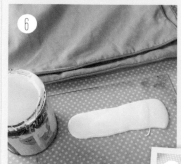

ALSO LOOKS GOOD ON ...

Throws: Try printing these blocks on a large piece of soft cotton or wool felt in a variety of colors to create a "patchwork" throw.

Lampshades: Follow the instructions on pages 64–66 to make a knit-print drum lampshade cover.

Upholstery: Cover large areas of fabric with squares of this knit print, then use it to make a window shade or to upholster dining chairs.

SHIMMERING SCALES NAPKINS

★ ★ ★ ★ ★ ★ ★ ★ ★ ★ ★ ★ ★ ★ ★ ★ ★ ★ ★ ★

SUPPLIES

40" x 40" square of linen, washed and ironed

Round smooth-edged plastic cookie cutter, 4" in diameter

Sharp knife

Gold and white printing inks

Palette knife

Glass plate

Brayer (ink roller)

MAKES 4 NAPKINS

Using three different shades of gold ink gives the printed scallops on these napkins an iridescent quality, like fish scales.

TO PREPARE THE NAPKINS AND SCALLOP

1 Cut the linen into four 20" squares, then fray the edges of the linen by pulling the loose threads away until there is a ¼" edge of fringe. If necessary, trim the square again. Lay one napkin on a flat surface.

TO PREPARE THE SCALLOP

2 Take the cookie cutter and place it face up on a flat surface. Press the knife down across the widest point of the cutter and cut straight down both sides of the plastic. Carefully cut away one half of the plastic until you are left with a semicircular scallop shape.

EXTRA!

Look out for different size scallop shapes that could be used for printing. The end caps of PVC drainpipes are a great size for printing larger-scale scallops ideal for pillows or wallpaper.

Print three or four rows of scallops all around the base of a tablecloth to match your napkins.

CONT. ⟩⟩⟩

TO PRINT ON THE NAPKINS

3 Prepare three shades of gold ink on the glass plate. One batch can be straight from the tube, the other two have different amounts of white mixed into them. For the lightest one, mix 2 parts white and 2 parts gold and for the mid shade mix 1 part white to 3 parts gold. Mix each one well with the palette knife and spread out quite thickly on the glass.

4 Start printing the napkin. Place the cookie cutter onto one shade of the gold, making sure there is a nice even coverage of ink on the scallop edge.

5 Place the scallop on the bottom left of the napkin and press down firmly. Carefully remove the scallop, ink up again and repeat, placing the scallop so it is touching the first one. After about three prints, change to the mid color of gold and print a few more, then use the lightest color.

6 Repeat until the first row of scallops is completed. Print row two by starting the scallop at the highest point of the first scallop in the first row. You will see the fish scale pattern begin to build up.

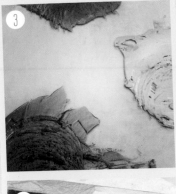

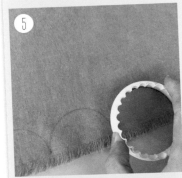

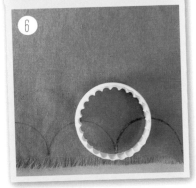

7 Complete this row by printing two half scallops at either end. Again change the color of the ink every so often. Try to do this in a random way, sometimes printing just one of each color and sometimes printing a run of three or four in one color. In this way, a lovely undulating pattern of light and shadow builds up. Continue printing the rows until the whole napkin is filled.

8 Repeat with each napkin and leave them to dry overnight.

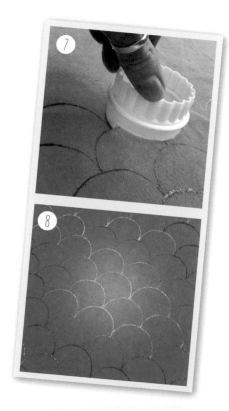

CHAPTER 2

LAZY LINO PRINTS

When I was younger I spent many hours warming brittle pieces of lino on a radiator before they were soft enough to scoop out intricate patterns, or I would chisel into fiberboard (and the tips of my fingers) to make wood cuts. Nowadays, block printing has gotten a lot more finger friendly with the arrival of safer, softer printing materials. All the projects in this chapter use craft foam, a thin polystyrene sheet, which is easy to cut with a knife or scissors and so easy to indent with a pencil. The effects you get can be just as intricate as a traditional lino or woodblock print, but in about a tenth of the time. The foam is also relatively cheap, so it doesn't matter if your pencil slips or you cut away the wrong piece, as you can just start again and be ready to print in no time.

- Bow Shoes • Nordic Forest Lampshade
- Nordic Forest Bag • Owl Family Notebooks
- Mrs. Hare and Family Tote Bag • Mrs. Hare T-shirt
- Mushroom Mayhem Pillow • Toadstool Pillow
- Bloomin' Marvelous Storage Boxes
- Raindrop Umbrella • Circus Letter Wooden Postcards

BOW SHOES

This is a quick and cute way of making a boring pair of canvas shoes fun and unique. You could also make smaller bows and print over the whole shoe.

Pencil

Sheet of craft foam

Masking tape

Cutting mat

Craft knife

Metal ruler

Thin cardboard

Pair of canvas shoes

Turquoise printing ink

Glass plate

Brayer (ink roller)

TO PREPARE THE PRINTING BLOCK

1 Using the bow template on page 117 and following steps 1–4 on pages 16–17, prepare a Lazy Lino bow. You are printing onto a curved surface so it is easier not to stick the bow to a clear plastic block base.

TO PRINT ON THE SHOES

2 Make two rough semicircles from the cardboard to place inside the toes of your shoes. This gives a firmer base to print onto.

3 Squeeze some of the turquoise ink onto the glass plate and roll it out to a fine consistency (see page 15). Roll the ink onto the Lazy Lino bow.

4 Carefully place the bow in position on the toe of the shoe.

5 Press down firmly on the Lazy Lino. You may find it helps to put one hand inside the shoe and press up from below as well. Make sure you press firmly and evenly over the whole bow.

6 Gently peel the bow away from the shoe. Repeat steps 2–6 on the other shoe. Leave overnight to dry fully.

NORDIC FOREST LAMPSHADE

This lampshade design is inspired by the misty Scandinavian conifer forests of Norway and Sweden, where the trees gradually fade into the sky. I love the magical way the trees light up when it is turned on.

TO PREPARE THE PRINTING BLOCKS

1. Using the templates on page 123 as a guide for design ideas and following the instructions on pages 16–17, prepare two clear plastic blocks with four trees on each—tree set A and tree set B.

TO PREPARE THE CARDSTOCK FOR THE LAMPSHADE

2. Using the tape measure, check the circumference and height of the lampshade. Cut out a rectangle of cardstock to these dimensions but add ³⁄₄" extra all around.

3. Lay the rectangle of cardstock horizontally on a flat surface.

TO PRINT ON THE LAMPSHADE

4. Mix up some beige ink on the glass plate and roll it out to a fine consistency (see page 15). Ink up the two tree blocks and wipe away any excess ink with a damp cloth.

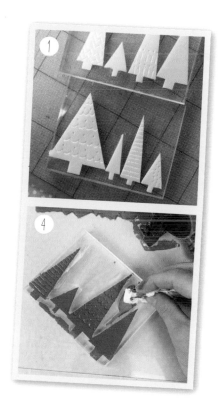

CONT. >>>

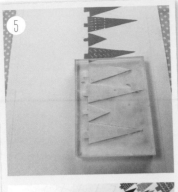

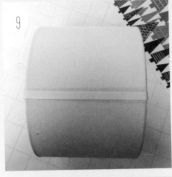

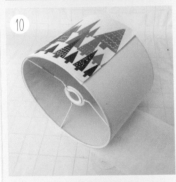

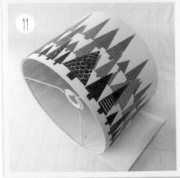

5 Begin printing at the top left of the cardstock so the tip of the tallest tree is 1" from the top. Print the first row of trees alternating the two blocks in a random pattern.

6 When this first row is finished, clean up the blocks with a damp cloth and pat dry.

7 Mix up the pink ink and roll out a thin layer. Ink up the blocks as before and print the next row of trees so they overlap the first by ⅓. Stagger the trees so that they sit in a different position to the first row. Again alternate the two blocks.

8 Clean up the blocks. Mix up the brown printing ink and print the final row as before, positioning the base a little more than ¾" from the bottom. Leave to dry.

9 Using a craft knife and metal ruler, neatly trim the rectangle, removing the excess ¾" of cardstock around the edge so it will exactly cover the lampshade. Take a strip of double-sided tape and run it along the vertical join of the lampshade from top to bottom. When the ink is dry, turn the cardstock over and run a strip of tape along the short side on the right-hand side.

10 Remove the protective strip from the tape on the lampshade and the cardstock. Place the lampshade in the middle of the design (making sure the trees are the right way up). Lift up the left-hand side of the cardstock rolling it around the lampshade and secure the end to the tape on the lampshade.

11 Roll the other side of the cardstock around the lampshade, keeping it tight to the lampshade. Secure it in place using the tape on the cardstock.

12 Place the completed lampshade on your chosen lampbase and switch on.

ALSO LOOKS GOOD ON ...

Wrapping paper: Try printing either rows or just individual copses of trees.

Pillow covers: Matching lampshade and pillow covers would look great in a living room.

Greeting cards: One block of these trees is the perfect size for a greeting card. For delightful Christmas cards, choose an appropriate color and add a sprinkling of glitter.

NORDIC FOREST BAG

The trees on this bag are the same ones as those used on the lampshade on pages 64–67. Instead of putting four trees on a clear plastic block at one time, stick each one on an individual block. The bag in these pictures uses seven of the different tree designs.

Lay the bag out on a flat surface and tape it down. Then mix up a light pink ink and print one tree randomly three or four times over the bag. Next mix up a dark gray and repeat with the second tree.

Repeat with light gray, olive, pale olive, and bright pink inks, building up little copses of trees all over the bag.

Leave the bag to dry overnight.

OWL FAMILY NOTEBOOKS

★ ★

I was inspired by the amazing tessellations by M.C. Escher when I was thinking up this project. Though my owls aren't quite as impressive as his illustrations, they do have a pleasing repeat pattern.

SUPPLIES

Pencil

Sheets of craft foam

Masking tape

Cutting mat

Craft knife

Metal ruler

Double-sided tape

Three clear plastic blocks

Turquoise, teal, and pale turquoise printing inks (see pages 12–13 for color mixing tips)

Palette knife

Glass plate

Three brayers (ink rollers)

Damp cloth

Baren or rolling pin

Notebooks with cardboard covers

TO PREPARE THE PRINTING BLOCKS

1. Using the templates on page 114 and following the instructions on pages 16–17, prepare three clear plastic blocks with an owl on each. Use owls A and B and only the solid block of owl C.

TO PRINT ON THE NOTEBOOK

2. Using a different brayer for each, roll out the three colors of ink on the same glass plate to a fine consistency (see page 15).

3. Make two practice prints before you start on the notebooks (see steps 12–14 on page 18). Then print owl A in turquoise in the middle of the notebook.

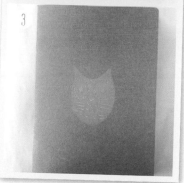

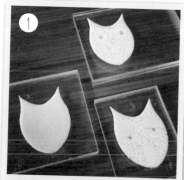

CONT. >>>

71

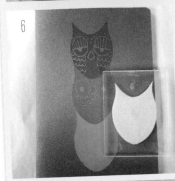

>>>

4 Print owl B in teal and position him, so that his tail is nestled between owl A's ears.

5 Print the solid block of owl C in the pale turquoise and nestle him beneath owl A.

6 Start printing the second row of owls with owl B. He should fit snugly in the right-hand curves created by owls A and C.

7 Repeat steps 4–6 until the whole book is covered.

8 Leave the book to dry. Meanwhile, clean off any excess ink from owl C, then draw the overprint details from page 114 onto it. Mix up some more teal ink and add a little white to it to make it paler. Use this to ink up owl C again. Print over the solid print on the book. Leave to dry.

ALSO LOOKS GOOD ON ...

Kids T-shirts: Enlarge the owl template and print one big owl in the middle of a T-shirt. You could print a back view of the owl on the reverse of the shirt.

Greeting cards: Cut a branch shape and a leaf shape to give your owl something to perch upon on the front of a set of greeting cards.

EXTRA!

To get the look shown in the main picture on page 70, print the owls with a slight border around each one. Just leave some space between each owl when printing. On smaller notebooks, use only one or two owls.

MRS. HARE AND FAMILY TOTE BAG

★ ★ ★ ★ ★ ★ ★ ★ ★ ★ ★ ★ ★ ★ ★ ★ ★ ★ ★ ★

I used to cover my school notebooks with doodles like the ones decorating Mrs. Hare and her children. They are very satisfying to draw. The hare shape looks great as a repeat pattern.

Pencil

Sheet of craft foam, 12" x 17"

Masking tape

Cutting mat

Craft knife

Metal ruler

Double-sided tape

Piece of thin fiberboard, for block base for Mrs. Hare (optional)

Three clear plastic blocks, for small hares

Gray, yellow, and white printing inks (see pages 12–13 for color mixing tips)

Glass plate

Brayer (ink roller)

Damp cloth

Baren or rolling pin

Gray cotton tote bag, washed and ironed

Piece of thin cardboard to put inside the bag (optional)

TO PREPARE THE PRINTING BLOCK

1 Using the large Mrs. Hare template on page 122 and following the instructions on pages 16–17, prepare the large hare block. After you have cut out Mrs. Hare from the foam, you need to draw in the pattern. You can either copy the pattern on the template using carbon paper (see page 14) or draw one freehand. Start by drawing a semicircle from her armpit to her mid thigh. Surround this with a scalloped line.

2 Then working out from this line draw circles of dots, dashes, hearts, or whatever you like until she is covered.

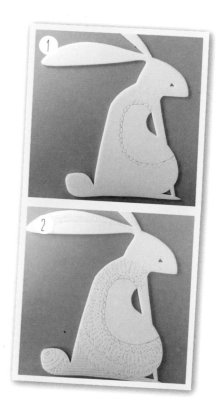

CONT. ⟩⟩⟩

3 Repeat with her ears and finally draw in her nose and whiskers.

4 Mrs. Hare is quite large, so you won't need a clear plastic block to print her with. If you are going to be printing several and you don't have a large enough plastic block, you may want to fasten her to a piece of thin fiberboard to make her more substantial.

TO PRINT ON THE TOTE BAG

5 Mix up some gray ink on the glass plate (you will find that you need more ink than usual for this large print) and roll it out to a fine consistency (see page 15). Ink up the hare and make a couple of test prints. Use a rolling pin to apply an even pressure.

6 Place the tote bag on a firm flat surface. If the bag is made of thin material, place a piece of cardboard inside so the ink doesn't bleed through.

7 Place the hare in the middle of the bag about 1¼" from the base and print (see steps 12–14 on page 18). Leave Mrs. Hare to dry.

8 Meanwhile, make up three of the small hares for the reverse of the bag, following steps 1–4 and using the small hare template on page 122. You need three blocks, one for each color of paint. Add the decorative patterns to one of them.

9 Print the patterned hare first in white, then print solid yellow hares, followed by gray hares. Use a baren or rolling pin to get an even pressure over the block. Leave to dry overnight.

ALSO LOOKS GOOD ON ...

T-shirts: The large hare fits perfectly on the front of a T-shirt or print a random pattern of little ones.

A wall frieze: An irregular line of these mini hares would make a cute frieze around the wall of a baby's room. Or print several onto cardstock and cut them out to make a mobile.

MRS. HARE T-SHIRT

Mrs. Hare is the perfect size for a T-shirt. Before you print, make sure you wash and iron the T-shirt.

To work out the best placement for the hare, put on the T-shirt and hold the foam block in front of you in a mirror. Move Mrs. Hare around until she looks like she's in the right place.

Make a little mark on the T-shirt with tailor's chalk or a pencil where you want the top of her ears to be. Lay the shirt on a flat surface, taping down the shoulders and bottom of the shirt.

Ink up Mrs. Hare as in step 5 on page 76, and print onto the shirt. Use a clean rolling pin to apply an even pressure.

MUSHROOM MAYHEM PILLOW

The slightly larger scale of these mushroom motifs and the fact that large areas of the foam is cut away gives a traditional rustic woodcut feel to the prints.

SUPPLIES

Pencil

Sheets of craft foam

Masking tape

Cutting mat

Craft knife

Metal ruler

Double-sided tape

Nine clear plastic blocks

Pillow cover, washed and ironed, and a pillow form

Piece of thin cardboard to put inside the pillow cover (optional)

Brown and white printing inks (see pages 12–13 for color mixing tips)

Palette knife

Glass plate

Two brayers (ink rollers)

Damp cloth

Baren or rolling pin

TO PREPARE THE PRINTING BLOCKS

1 Using the templates on page 115 and following the instructions on pages 16–17, prepare seven clear plastic blocks with a mushroom on each—the outlines of mushrooms A–F. If you don't have a plastic block large enough for mushroom B, don't worry as this piece of foam is big enough to print from directly.

2 Prepare two more blocks—for the white bases for mushrooms A and C. The brown outline will be printed over the white base on these two mushrooms.

CONT. >>>

TO PRINT ON THE PILLOW COVER

3 Lay the pillow cover on a flat surface. If the cover is thin, place cardboard inside so the ink doesn't soak through.

4 Mix up some brown ink on the glass plate and roll it out to a fine consistency (see page 15). Begin printing with mushroom E (see steps 12–14 on page 18). Print three or four mushrooms over the cover, making sure they are all at different angles to each other.

5 Start building up a pattern around the mushrooms, filling in the spaces between larger mushrooms with smaller ones.

6 Roll out the white ink to a fine consistency and print the base color for mushrooms A and C.

7 Don't worry about keeping all the mushrooms contained within the pillow cover; print some over the sides.

8 When you have filled the cover, the white ink will have dried, so now you can print the brown outline block for mushrooms A and C over the top of the white.

9 Leave the cover to dry overnight before you fill it with a pillow form and put it on a chair.

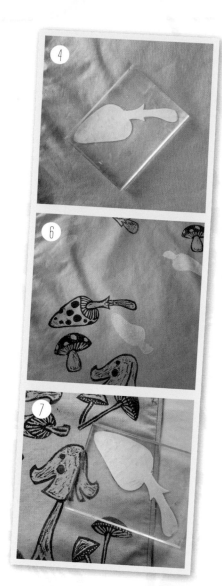

ALSO LOOKS GOOD ON …

A lampshade: Print a random pattern of mushrooms on a lampshade (see pages 64–67) to make a matching set.

The base of a wall: Clusters of mushrooms around the base of a wall in a summerhouse or hallway would add interest to an otherwise plain wall.

Notebooks and greeting cards: Individual mushrooms printed on stationery make an attractive gift set.

TOADSTOOL PILLOW

In this project, I show you how to overprint different blocks to build up a multicolored image. I have used two shades of pink together with red, white, and brown, but the end result would be equally effective in just red, white, and brown.

SUPPLIES

Pencil

Sheets of craft foam

Masking tape

Cutting mat

Craft knife

White, pink, red, and brown printing inks (see pages 12–13 for color mixing tips)

Glass plate

Two brayers (ink rollers)

16" square pillow cover, washed and ironed, and a pillow form

TO PREPARE THE PRINTING BLOCKS

1. Using the templates on pages 120–121 and following the instructions on pages 16–17, prepare a foam piece for each of the toadstool outlines. As the toadstool pieces are all quite large, you don't need clear plastic blocks to print with.

2. Prepare a separate piece of foam for each toadstool base color. The outlines are printed over the base colors.

TO PRINT ON THE PILLOW COVER

3. Squeeze some white ink on the glass plate and roll it out to a fine consistency (see page 15). Print the three white toadstool stalks. Use a clean brayer to apply even pressure over the back of the foam.

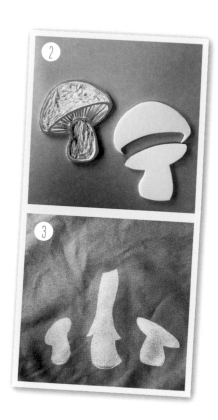

CONT. >>>

》》》

4 Add a little red to the white ink and mix it together well to make a pale pink for the cap of toadstool C. Roll the ink onto the foam and carefully position it in place above the white stalk.

5 Add a little more red to the ink to make a slightly darker pink. Use the ink to repeat step 4 for the cap of toadstool B.

6 Repeat step 4 for the cap of toadstool A and the spots of toadstool B, but this time use a neat red ink for the color.

7 Ideally leave these colors to dry before you print the outlines.

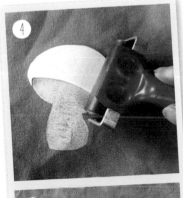

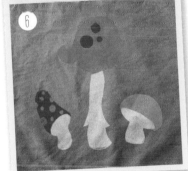

8 Mix up some brown ink and roll it out to a fine consistency, then roll the ink onto one of the toadstool outlines. Carefully position the foam on top of the colored ink shapes and apply an even pressure to the back of the foam.

9 Remove the foam block to reveal the toadstool outline. Repeat for other toadstools.

10 Leave the cover to dry overnight before you fill it with a pillow form and admire your work.

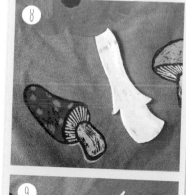

ALSO LOOKS GOOD ON ...

A raincoat: Use a single image on each pocket or, if you want, print a pattern all around the hem. For a larger repeat pattern, mix these toadstools with the mushrooms on pages 78–81.

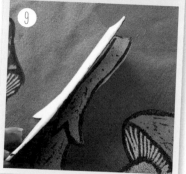

BLOOMIN' MARVELOUS STORAGE BOXES

These pretty flowers will liven up any plain storage or gift box. Give old shoeboxes a new lease on life or spruce up your tin kitchen containers.

SUPPLIES

Pencil

Sheets of craft foam

Masking tape

Cutting mat

Craft knife

Double-sided tape

Four clear plastic blocks

White, lilac, red, and gray printing inks (see pages 12–13 for color mixing tips)

Glass plate

Brayer (ink roller)

Damp cloth

Glass plate

Baren or rolling pin

Plain storage boxes

Wooden pencil with eraser

TO PREPARE THE PRINTING BLOCKS

1 Using the templates on page 117 and following the instructions on pages 16–17 prepare the foam flower shapes for printing.

2 Use a pencil to engrave the patterns on the foam pieces.

3 Mount the four foam pieces that are marked to be printed in white onto clear plastic blocks.

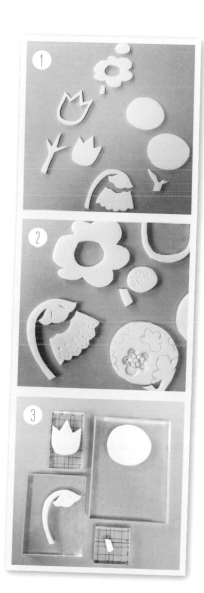

CONT. >>>

》》》

TO PRINT ON THE STORAGE BOXES

4 Squeeze some white ink onto the glass plate and roll it out to a fine consistency (see page 15). Ink up each clear plastic block and print onto the top of the box and around the sides, or wherever you like (see steps 12–14 on page 18).

5 Remove the pieces of foam from the plastic blocks and clean them up (see page 14). Then mount the two flower pieces that are going to be printed in lilac. Mix up the lilac ink, ink up the blocks, and print the lilac areas.

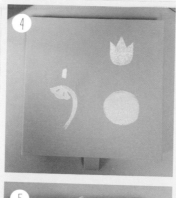

6 Repeat step 5 for the three gray pieces of the flowers.

7 Then repeat step 5 for the two red pieces of the flowers. Use the eraser end of a wooden pencil to make the small red dots for the gray flower. Leave to dry.

ALSO LOOKS GOOD ON ...

Greeting cards: Print one flower on each card to make pretty sets to give as presents.

Office supplies: Liven up your office space with some bright blooms. Print a random repeat pattern over plain box files, folders, and notebooks.

RAINDROP UMBRELLA

★ ★ ★ ★ ★ ★ ★ ★ ★ ★ ★ ★ ★ ★ ★ ★ ★ ★

I always think it's sad that most umbrellas have the pretty print only on the outside so the person hiding beneath it doesn't get to see it. This one has prints on both sides, so everyone's a winner.

SUPPLIES

Pencil

Sheets of craft foam

Masking tape

Cutting mat

Craft knife

Double-sided tape

Three clear plastic blocks

Plain umbrella

White, turquoise, and silver printing inks (see pages 12–13 for color mixing tips)

Palette knife

Glass plate

Brayer (ink roller)

Baren or rolling pin

TO PREPARE THE PRINTING BLOCKS

1 Using the templates on page 116 and following the instructions on pages 16–17, prepare three clear plastic blocks with a cloud on each.

TO PRINT ON THE UMBRELLA

2 Squeeze out some white ink on the glass plate and roll it out to a fine consistency (see page 15). Ink up the first cloud.

3 Open your umbrella (if you're superstitious you may want to do this part outside!) and print the cloud on the inside of one of the segments (see steps 12–14 on page 18). Repeat in each of the segments, printing the cloud in a different place each time.

CONT. >>>

〉〉〉

4 Repeat with the other two clouds. Mix up a fine consistency of pale turquoise for one cloud and a silvery blue for the other. Again print the clouds in different positions on each segment, sometimes overlapping them. Leave the umbrella open to dry.

5 Prepare the raindrops. To ensure the raindrops fit under the cloud, print one of each cloud onto a piece of scrap paper. Then cut out the raindrops from the foam using the templates on page 116. Stick double-sided tape to the back of each of them and place the raindrops for one of the clouds face down on the paper in the position you want them to be printed in.

6 Remove the clouds from the plastic blocks and clean the blocks to reuse them. Then place a clear plastic block on top of the raindrop arrangement and press down so they stick to the block.

7 This time working on the outside of the umbrella, print the raindrops adjacent to their corresponding cloud (you will be able to see the cloud clearly through the fabric).

8 Repeat steps 5–7 with the other two clouds and their raindrops. Leave the umbrella open to dry.

ALSO LOOKS GOOD ON ...

Notebooks: Print just one cloud in a repeat pattern over both the front and back of the notebook.

Pillow covers: If you cut out a circle and print it in yellow, you can make a lovely rain and shine pattern for the center of a pillow cover.

Duvet set: Over-sized clouds make a lovely repeat pattern across a duvet cover. You could then also print a large yellow sun on a pillowcase to make a cool bedding set.

CIRCUS LETTER WOODEN POSTCARDS

SUPPLIES

Sheets of craft foam

Masking tape

Cutting mat

Craft knife

Double-sided tape

Clear plastic blocks

Wooden postcards, 6" x 4"

Assorted colors of printing inks (see pages 12–13 for color mixing tips)

One brayer (ink roller) for each color of ink

Glass plate

Wooden pencil with eraser

Assorted colors of rubber stamp inks

Star-shaped rubber stamp (optional)

EXTRA!
You can buy blank wooden postcards online, but they are expensive. For a less expensive alternative, buy a sheet of ¼" plywood and cut several 6" x 4" rectangles from it. Sand down the edges until they are smooth.

I adore circus lettering and these initial postcards are a lovely modern take on personalized stationery. The postcards make great wedding invitations or baby announcements.

TO PREPARE THE PRINTING BLOCKS AND WOODEN POSTCARDS

1 Choose your preferred letters from the templates on pages 124–125 and, following the instructions on pages 16–17, cut the letters from the foam and secure each one to a clear plastic block. Use two foam letter shapes for each initial: a larger one for the three-dimensional effect base shape and a smaller one to print over the top.

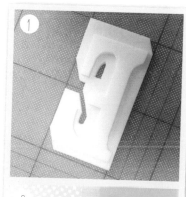

2 Print a square of base color on the wooden postcard by rolling out the desired color ink. Push the brayer over the wood. Leave the ink to dry.

TO PRINT THE LETTERS ON THE POSTCARDS

3 Mix your chosen color for the larger letter block on the glass plate and roll it out to a thin consistency (see page 15). Transfer the ink onto the letter.

CONT. >>>

〉〉〉

4 Place the clear plastic block centrally on the wooden postcard. Roll over the block with a clean brayer to apply a firm and even pressure. Carefully remove the block and leave the ink to dry.

5 To add stripes or any other patterns inside the smaller letter, use a pencil to draw directly onto the foam (see page 14 for further instructions). Then repeat steps 2–4 for the second slightly smaller initial using a contrasting color. Make sure you position this block in the correct place on top of the larger initial.

6 To create the decorative dots around the edges of the letters, use the eraser end of a wooden pencil and ink from a rubber stamp pad. Alternatively, further decorate the postcards using small store-bought rubber stamps or cut your own shapes from the foam sheet.

ALSO LOOKS GOOD ON ...

Greeting cards: If you can't easily get hold of or make your own wooden postcards then blank greeting cards work just as well. To print a pair of initials onto one card, just cut each letter slightly smaller than suggested for this project.

Framed prints: Use a selection of letters printed onto art paper to make up favorite words or names.

Pillow covers: Enlarge an initial to fill a pillow cover and print directly onto the fabric.

CHAPTER 3

OTHER PRINTING TECHNIQUES

You don't just have to use a found object or cut
a block to make beautiful patterns and prints.
This chapter has projects that use the sun, a ball
of string, bleach, and white craft glue to make
a variety of effective and professional-looking
printed items. One of my favorite projects in the
book is in this chapter, the Bleach Beach Towels
(see page 104). I was so pleased with
the results that every towel I own now has
some sort of print on it.

• Ginkgo Leaf Shade • Bleach Beach Towels
• "Which Way?" Pencil Case • Sunflower Tablecloth

GINKGO LEAF SHADE

★ ★

Two different techniques are used to make the blocks for this shade.
One gives a solid leaf print and the other shows the more delicate veins
in the leaf by using good old-fashioned string stuck to the foam sheet.

SUPPLIES

Pencil

Sheet of craft foam, 12" x 17"

Masking tape

Cutting mat

Craft knife

Thick, stiff cardboard

White craft glue

Old paintbrush

String or garden twine

Scissors

Green, yellow, and white printing inks
(see pages 12–13 for color mixing tips)

Glass sheet

Brayer (ink roller)

Rolling pin

White or pale color roller shade

TO MAKE THE PRINTING BLOCKS

1 Using the templates on pages 118–119 and following the instructions on pages 16–17, cut two leaf shapes from the foam sheet.

2 Choose one of the templates to be the string skeleton leaf block and draw around it onto the piece of cardboard.

3 Cover the cardboard with a thick layer of white craft glue. Take a length of string and coat this in the glue. Place the string on the cardboard, following the outline of the leaf and pressing down with your fingers. (If the string isn't staying in place, leave the glue to thicken slightly, then try again.)

4 Draw lines for the veins on the cardboard. Then cut lengths of string and place them on the veins.

5 Coat the whole block with more glue, using an old paintbrush and a downward dabbing motion.

CONT. >>>

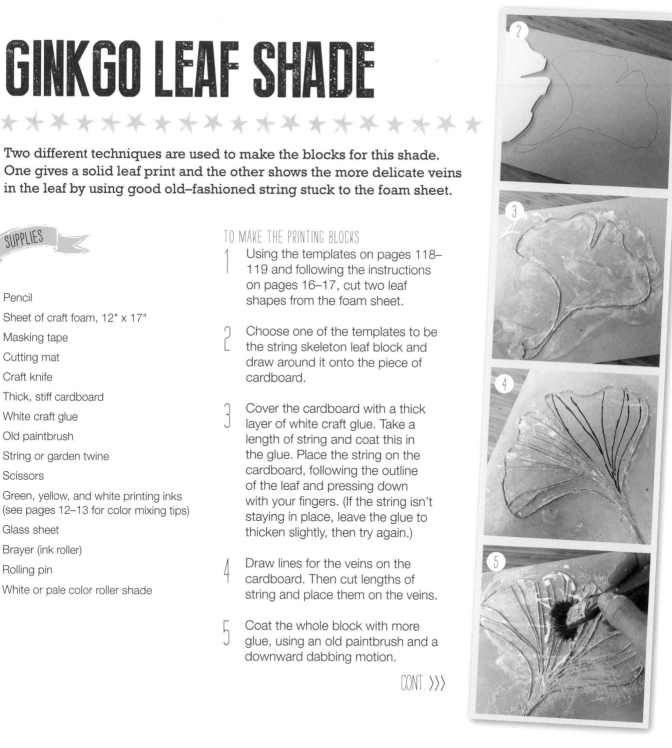

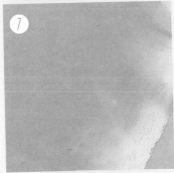

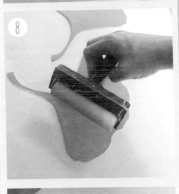

>>>

6 Leave the string block to dry, ideally overnight or at least until all the glue has gone clear. Cut away the excess cardboard, leaving the leaf shape.

TO PRINT ON THE SHADE

7 Print the solid green leaves first. Mix up a greeny yellow on the glass plate using 2 parts green and 1 part yellow. Roll out to a fine consistency (see page 15), but don't completely mix the color together. For a more realistic look, it's better to leave the paint mix so it is a little patchy.

8 Roll the ink onto the foam blocks, trying to keep the yellow part of the brayer on the edge of the leaf.

9 Lay the shade out on a flat surface over a protective covering on your table. It's best if you can lay out the whole length of the shade at once. Starting at the bottom of the shade, begin printing the leaves. As you print each leaf, rotate them so they look like they are falling. Alternate the two leaf shapes and print some over the edges of the shade. Remember to leave space for the white string skeleton leaf.

10 For the white skeleton leaf, squeeze out some white ink on the glass plate and roll out to a medium consistency. Ink up the string block and make a couple of practice prints on some scraps of paper or fabric, as the ink takes a while to soak into the string.

11 Print the white skeleton leaves in between the green ones, rotating them as before. Leave to dry overnight.

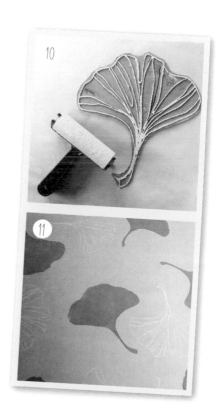

BLEACH BEACH TOWELS

These towels look so professional and the pattern is so complicated it's hard to believe they are simply done with household bleach and a cookie cutter. Cutters of any shape can be used, and once you've got the hang of it you can make random or geometric patterns super quickly.

SUPPLIES

Towel, washed and ironed

Large plastic sheet

Heavy-duty masking tape or duct tape

Rubber gloves

Thick household bleach

Glass, metal, or ceramic flat-bottomed bowl

Cookie cutters in your chosen shape and size—for the turquoise towel, I used a circular cutter; for the light blue towel, I used a six-pointed star; and for the dark blue towel, a triangle cutter (see page 106)

BEFORE PRINTING ...

It is best to practice this technique with a washcloth in the same terry cloth first so you get the hang of how drippy the bleach is and what color the towel will turn when bleached.

TO PREPARE FOR PRINTING

1 Prepare your work area: bleach will not only strip out the color from your towels, but also from any other fabric it touches, so make sure you're wearing old clothes and protect the area around you with a large plastic sheet. I tend to do any bleach printing outdoors, as it's less risky. Bleach doesn't strip the color out right away, so you won't notice the massive splash marks on your favorite pillow or tablecloth until it's too late!

2 Lay the towel in a landscape position on a protected flat surface—an old piece of wood slightly larger than the towel is good or a tabletop protected by plastic.

3 Tape the towel to the surface along all its sides. Try to just tape the bound selvage of the towel and not the fluffy loops. Also cover with tape any part of the towel that you don't want bleached.

4 Put on the rubber gloves and pour bleach into the bowl to a depth of 1/2". Place the bowl near your towel and put the cookie cutter in the bleach.

CONT. >>>

TO PRINT THE PATTERN

5 Lift out the cookie cutter and hold it above the bowl for 5 seconds to allow any excess bleach to drain off. Some shapes may create a film of bleach across the cutter. If a bubble forms, pop it with your finger (if doing this project with children: get them to wear safety glasses).

6 Starting at the bottom left of the towel, place the cutter in position and press onto the towel as firmly as if you were cutting out a cookie.

7 Remove the cutter from the towel, dip it back in the bleach and repeat step 6 until the towel is covered.

8 You will notice the bleach develops over time—the longer you leave it, the paler the bleached areas will go. Wait until the towel is completely dry (and the bleach has done its work), then hand wash with a mild detergent. Hang the towel out to dry.

TO MAKE THE OTHER TWO TOWELS ...

Follow steps 1–5 to prepare the towels, then print.

To print triangles on the dark blue towel
ROW 1: With the triangular cookie cutter, print one row of triangles along the bottom width of the towel.

ROW 2: Print another row of triangles directly above the first so the base of the second row touches the tip of the first. Repeat until finished and then follow step 8.

To print stars on the light blue towel
ROW 1: With the star cookie cutter, print one row of stars with one star point at the top and one at the bottom. Make sure the adjacent stars touch each other.

ROW 2: Print the second row above the first, again making sure the lower points of the second row touch the upper points of the first. Repeat until finished and then follow step 8.

"WHICH WAY?" PENCIL CASE

This project is made from a product called Inkodye, which uses good old sunshine to make it work. You also need a shaped hole punch: I have used one shaped like an arrow, but there are many other shapes you could choose from.

SUPPLIES

Light-colored cotton pencil case

Arrow-shaped hole punch

Black paper

Inkodye kit (see page 126)

Glass plate

Sunshine

1 Wash the pencil case and leave it to dry completely. Use the hole punch to punch out 40 or so arrows from the black paper.

2 Place the case on a tray, then follow the instructions from the Inkodye kit and cover the front of the pencil case with the dye using the brayer sponge that comes with the kit. Throw away any excess dye.

3 Scatter the arrow shapes over the pencil case, pressing each one down onto the ink to stay in place.

4 Put the glass over the case and take it and the tray outside into the sunshine. You will see the ink change color immediately.

5 After 20 minutes (or when you think the color can't go any darker), bring the case indoors. Remove the black arrows to reveal the original color of the case.

6 Repeat with the back of the case, if required, and then follow the kit instructions for washing and drying it, so it's all ready to be filled.

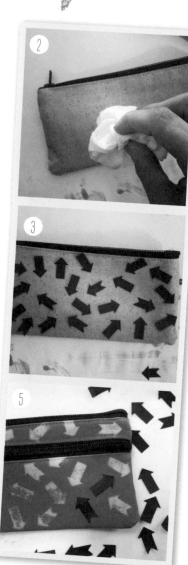

SUNFLOWER TABLECLOTH

★ ★ ★ ★ ★ ★ ★ ★ ★ ★ ★ ★ ★ ★ ★ ★ ★ ★ ★ ★

The big bountiful blooms of these sunflowers make a cheery print for a tablecloth or pillow. When making the printing block, the free-running glue makes for a charmingly relaxed abstract print.

SUPPLIES

Thick, stiff cardboard

Pen

Bottle of white craft glue with a nozzle top

Scissors or craft knife and cutting mat

Pale-colored round tablecloth

Ocher, orange, yellow, and green printing inks (see pages 12–13 for color mixing tips)

Glass sheet

Brayer (ink roller)

Rolling pin

TO PREPARE THE PRINTING BLOCKS

1. Using the sunflower drawings below left for inspiration, draw a rough sunflower shape onto the cardboard approximately 12" in diameter.

2. Using the glue nozzle as the drawing tool, squeeze glue through the nozzle following the sunflower shape. Aim for a consistent flow of glue around the flower (you can always fill in empty spaces later).

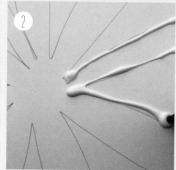

3. Complete the whole outline of the flower. If you aren't happy with the line, it is easy to wipe away with a damp cloth and try again until you get it right.

4. Repeat steps 1–3 to make two more flowers, each one a slightly different shape. Leave to dry, ideally overnight but at least until all the glue has gone clear. Cut out the flower around the glue with the scissors or craft knife, leaving 1/8–1/4" clear around the edge.

CONT. ⟩⟩⟩

>>>

5 Lay the tablecloth on a flat surface—a dining table or hard wood floor is ideal.

6 Mix up some ocher ink on the glass plate and roll it out to a medium consistency (see page 15). Then roll up one of the flowers. Clean away any excess ink on the block using a tissue (a little excess ink gives a nice texture to the print so don't worry if you don't get it all).

7 Place the flower block face down on the tablecloth about 2" up from the hem, press down and then use a clean rolling pin to apply pressure.

8 Carefully remove the block and re-ink it. Repeat step 7, moving the flower around the tablecloth and leaving about 4" between flowers until you have completed the circle.

9 Repeat steps 6–8 with the second sunflower block and using orange ink. Place it between two ocher flowers so just the tips of the petals are touching the tops of the ocher flowers. Leave room between the orange flowers for the third flower.

10 Repeat steps 6–8 with the third sunflower, printing this in yellow. Nestle it between the orange and ocher flowers.

11 Clean up the first flower and re-ink it with a green ink. Use this to print a border around the base of the tablecloth. Finally, print one sunflower in the middle of the tablecloth. Leave to dry.

ALSO LOOKS GOOD ON ...

Duvet cover: These flowers printed in shades of one color would liven up a dull bedroom. Either print all over the cover or just a band around the center.

Pillow cover or bag: Print either one big flower in the middle or cover completely in blooms.

Walls: A wall printed with oversize sunflowers would look amazing. Use 22" x 33" pieces of cardboard to make the blocks. When it comes to the printing, it is easiest to have two people around when printing onto the wall—one to hold the block on the wall and the other to apply the pressure. Fun!

TEMPLATES

OWL FAMILY NOTEBOOKS
Pages 70–73; use at 100%.

OWL C
OVERPRINT

OWL A

OWL C
SOLID BLOCK

OWL B

MUSHROOM MAYHEM PILLOW
Pages 78–81; use at 100%.

MUSHROOM A
OUTLINE

MUSHROOM F
OUTLINE

MUSHROOM B
OUTLINE

MUSHROOM A
Print in white.

MUSHROOM C
OUTLINE

MUSHROOM E
OUTLINE

MUSHROOM C
Print in white.

MUSHROOM D
OUTLINE

RAINDROP UMBRELLA

Pages 90–93; use at 100%.

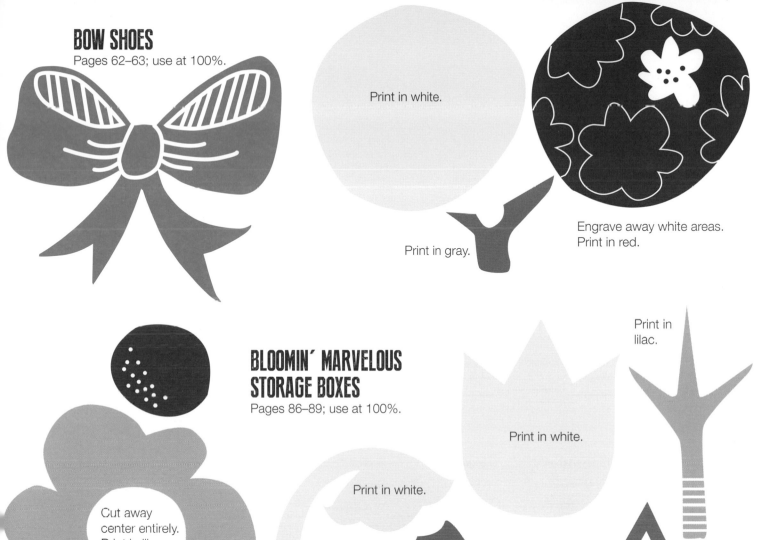

BOW SHOES
Pages 62–63; use at 100%.

Print in white.

Print in gray.

Engrave away white areas.
Print in red.

Print in lilac.

BLOOMIN' MARVELOUS STORAGE BOXES
Pages 86–89; use at 100%.

Print in white.

Cut away center entirely.
Print in lilac.

Print in white.

Print in white.

Cut away center entirely.
Print in gray.

Engrave away white areas.
Print in gray.

Print in white.

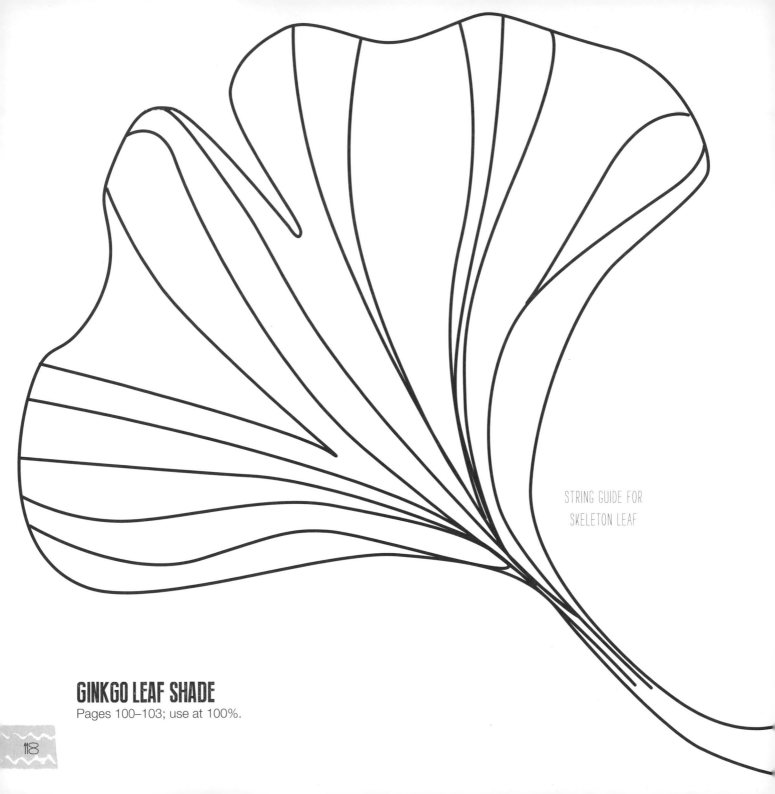

STRING GUIDE FOR
SKELETON LEAF

GINKGO LEAF SHADE

Pages 100–103; use at 100%.

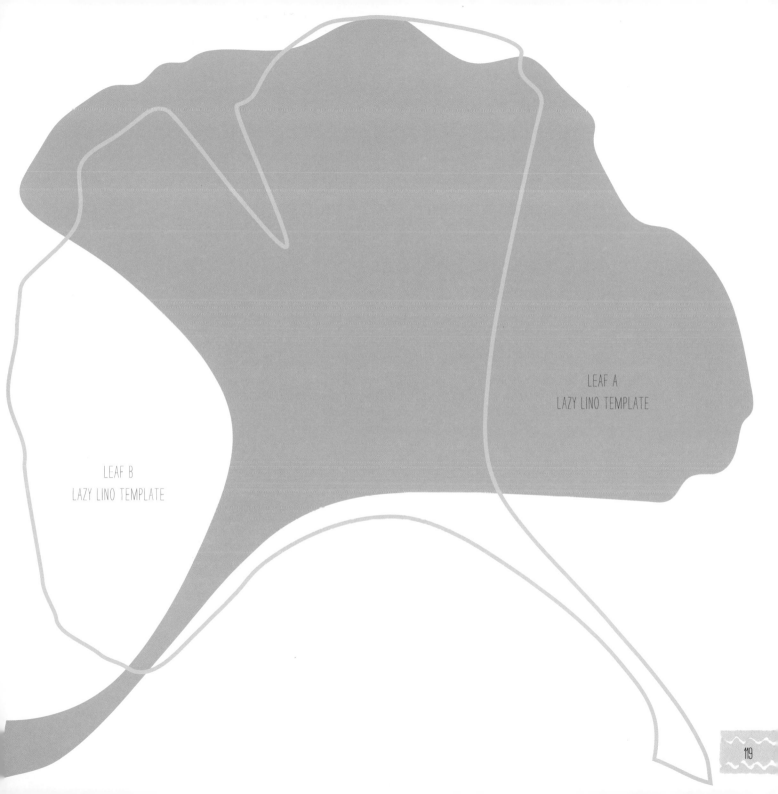

LEAF A
LAZY LINO TEMPLATE

LEAF B
LAZY LINO TEMPLATE

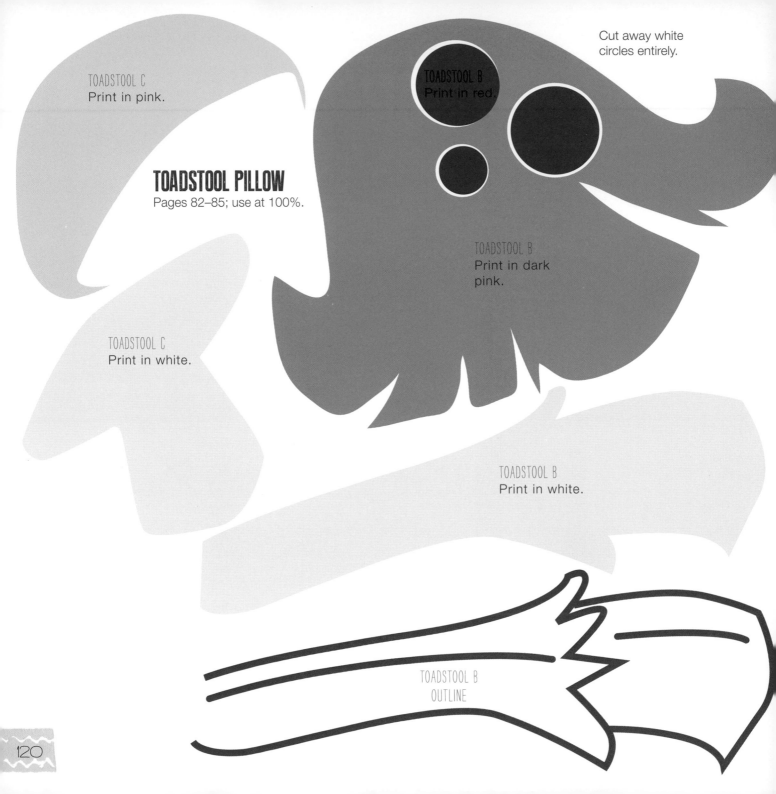

TOADSTOOL C
Print in pink.

TOADSTOOL B
Print in red.

Cut away white
circles entirely.

TOADSTOOL PILLOW
Pages 82–85; use at 100%.

TOADSTOOL B
Print in dark
pink.

TOADSTOOL C
Print in white.

TOADSTOOL B
Print in white.

TOADSTOOL B
OUTLINE

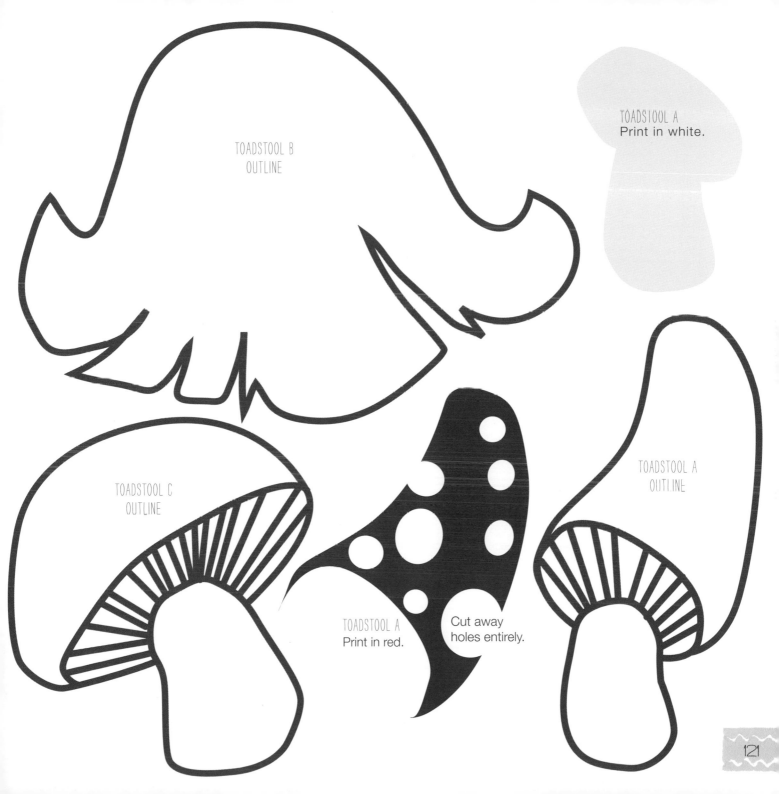

TOADSTOOL B
OUTLINE

TOADSTOOL A
Print in white.

TOADSTOOL C
OUTLINE

TOADSTOOL A
OUTLINE

TOADSTOOL A
Print in red.

Cut away
holes entirely.

121

MRS. HARE
Pages 74–77; enlarge by 150% for front of tote bag and T-shirt.

SMALL HARE
Pages 74–76; use at 100% for reverse of bag.

TREE SET A

TREE SET B

A B C D E
F G H I J
K L M N O

PQRST
UVWXY
ZØÆ★

**CIRCUS LETTER
WOODEN POSTCARDS**
Pages 94–97; enlarge by 170%.

SUPPLIERS

Craft foam sheets (Lazy Lino)

Sheets of craft foam are available from most craft stores and come in a range of sizes. This thin polystyrene foam is 3–6 mm thick. If searching online, look for "craft foam" or "scratch foam." I use foam sheets by Safeprint in the U.K.

Block printing inks

Try your local craft store for printing inks. I use fabric block printing inks by Speedball, which are suitable for fabric and paper (see page 9).

SPEEDBALL ART

Manufacturers of printing supplies and inks that can be found in all good art stores. Their website has a store locator and is full of helpful information on their products including a FAQ section where you can post any queries you have about a product or process.
www.speedballart.com

Palette knives for mixing inks

An artist's palette knife (a flexible metal spatula) is the professional printmaker's tool for mixing colors; this is available in art supply stores. For an inexpensive alternative mixing tool, try a narrow frosting spatula from a kitchen supply store.

Brayers (ink rollers) & barens

If you buy an inexpensive printing kit at a craft store, a brayer and a baren will be included. But if you get hooked on printing and want some more professional ink rollers and a traditional Japanese baren, try McClain's Printmaking Supplies at:
www.imcclains.com

General printmaking tools, materials, & inks

For second-hand printmaking tools, try eBay, where I bought several of my clear plastic (plexiglas) blocks for mounting Lazy Lino on.
Your local craft store will also have block printing tools and equipment. For purchasing tools and equipment online, try the following:
www.dickblick.com
www.speedballart.com

Fabric items to print on

For plain T-shirts, canvas shoes, pillow covers, bags, lampshades, hand and bath towels, dishtowels, napkins, and tablecloths just waiting to be printed on, try charity shops or inexpensive stores, such as Ikea or Walmart.
www.ikea.com/us
www.walmart.com

Inkodye kits

To buy Inkodye kits directly from the manufacturer, go to the Lumi website:
http://store.lumi.co/

Printmaking information

HANDPRINTED

This website is a one-stop shop for printing supplies in the UK. It sells everything you need for all kinds of printing. It also has several handy guides to printing to download and inspirational videos to watch.
www.handprinted.net

Free online fonts

For letters or shapes for your printing projects, you will find that there are lots of websites with free fonts to download. Try:
www.dafont.com
www.fontsquirrel.com

INDEX

THANK YOU THANK YOU THANK YOU

Thanks to all at Quadrille:
Lisa for accepting my million half-cocked emails without a murmur, and Gemma for making the book look ace. Thank you to Emma for making sure everything is spelt right and makes sense. To lovely Keiko for the beautifulness and to Chinh for looking so pretty.

Thank you to Miss Jones, who may or may not have come up with the book's title.

Thank you, too, to Speedball Art for supplying the inks and rollers for the book.

To all my family: Mum and Dad for their general brilliance, patience, and tidying skills; Jo, Ian, and the boys for their ideas and support; Aunty and Uncle; and Nanny and Grandad for their support, belief, encouragement, and suggestions.

Love to Jake, Kirsty (and Daisy now), Laura, and everyone who has to hear about "the book," even though half of you don't know which one I'm talking about now!

Publishing Director Jane O'Shea
Commissioning Editor Lisa Pendreigh
Editor Emma Callery
Creative Director Helen Lewis
Art Direction & Design Claire Peters
Designer Gemma Hogan
Photographer Keiko Oikawa
Stylist and Illustrator Christine Leech
Production Director Vincent Smith
Production Controller Aysun Hughes

Quadrille
craft

www.quadrillecraft.com

First edition for North America published in 2015 by Barron's Educational Series, Inc.

First published in 2014 by Quadrille Publishing Ltd.
Pentagon House
52–54 Southwark Street
London SE1 1UN
www.quadrille.co.uk

Text, projects, designs, artwork & illustrations
© 2014 Christine Leech
Photography
© 2014 Keiko Oikawa
Design & layout
© 2014 Quadrille Publishing Ltd.

All inquiries should be addressed to:
Barron's Educational Series, Inc.
250 Wireless Boulevard
Hauppauge, NY 11788
www.barronseduc.com

ISBN: 978-1-4380-0596-6

Library of Congress Control No.: 2014951246

Printed in China.

9 8 7 6 5 4 3 2 1